CAPE ✦ MAY

PERSPECTIVES

JACK & OLETA NEITH

Schiffer Publishing Ltd®

4880 Lower Valley Road · Atglen, Pennsylvania 19310

Other Schiffer Books by the Authors:
Great Kitchens, 978-0-7643-3008-7, $29.99
*Power Rooms: Executive Offices, Corporate Lobbies,
and Conference Rooms,* 978-0-7643-2920-3, $49.95

Other Schiffer Books on Related Subjects:
Cape May Lighthouse, 978-0-7643-3800-7, $9.99
Cape May Walking Tours, 978-0-7643-2946-3, $12.95
Cape May's Gingerbread Gems, 0-7643-2126-9, $9.95
Greetings from Cape May, 978-0-7643-2678-3, $19.95

Schiffer Books are available at special discounts for bulk purchases for sales promotions or premiums. Special editions, including personalized covers, corporate imprints, and excerpts can be created in large quantities for special needs. For more information contact the publisher:

Published by Schiffer Publishing Ltd.
4880 Lower Valley Road
Atglen, PA 19310
Phone: (610) 593-1777; Fax: (610) 593-2002
E-mail: Info@schifferbooks.com

For the largest selection of fine reference books on this and related subjects, please visit our web site at:
www.schifferbooks.com
We are always looking for people to write books on new and related subjects. If you have an idea for a book please contact us at the above address.

This book may be purchased from the publisher.
Include $5.00 for shipping.
Please try your bookstore first.
You may write for a free catalog.

In Europe, Schiffer books are distributed by
Bushwood Books
6 Marksbury Ave.
Kew Gardens
Surrey TW9 4JF England
Phone: 44 (0) 20 8392 8585; Fax: 44 (0) 20 8392 9876
E-mail: info@bushwoodbooks.co.uk
Website: www.bushwoodbooks.co.uk

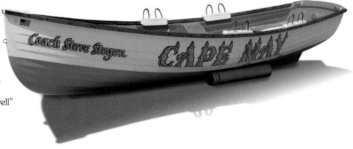

Designed by RoS
Type set in Nadall/Souvenir Lt BT

ISBN: 978-0-7643-3504-4
Printed in China

Contents

INTRODUCTION

Cape May, New Jersey, is famous for its Victorian heritage. This city, at the southern tip of Cape May Peninsula, is where the Delaware Bay meets the Atlantic Ocean. The earliest inhabitants of the peninsula were the Kechemeche Indians of the Lenni-Lenape tribe. They mainly hunted these grounds. After the sighting by Sir Henry Hudson in 1609, Cornelius Jacobson Mey explored the area in 1621. A prosperous fishing and whaling industry developed after the first residents purchased land from the Indians in the 1630s. By the late seventeenth century, English colonists from Connecticut and Massachusetts introduced farming in this area.

Cape May was originally formed by an Act of the New Jersey Legislature on March 8, 1848 as Cape Island. On March 10, 1851, it was reincorporated as Cape Island City. Cape May City, as we know it today, was formed on March 9, 1869. In the mid-1700s, Cape May began hosting visitors from Philadelphia. They came by schooners, stagecoaches, and horse-drawn wagons. At that time they were housed in rustic taverns, residents' homes, and public houses. The United States Government recognizes Cape May as the country's oldest seaside resort.

Hundreds of beautiful Victorian homes line the quaint streets in a rainbow of colors. Cape May has the second largest collection of Victorian-era homes in the country after San Francisco, California. Visitors can enjoy these homes with guided scenic trolley, walking, and horse-drawn carriage tours. Cape May is a year-round resort with numerous Bed and Breakfasts, restaurants, and activities. It hosts theme weekends throughout the year, including an autumn Tulip Festival, "Christmas in Cape May," Spring and Fall Jazz Festivals, professional theatre productions, art exhibits, and antique and crafts shows.

In 1970, the Emlen Physick estate was saved from demolition by a group of citizens who formed the Mid-Atlantic Center for The Arts (MAC) organization. Today, it operates two historic sites in Cape May: The Emlen Physick Estate and the Cape May Lighthouse.

• The Emlen Physick Estate is Cape May's only Victorian House Museum. It was built in 1879 and is attributed to the architect Frank Furness. The eighteen-room museum is decorated with authentic furniture, artwork, clothing, and personal items of Emlen Physick. Changing seasonal exhibits provide a glimpse into the daily lives of Emlen Physick and his family in this Victorian household.

• The Cape May Lighthouse, built in 1859, is one of the oldest continually operating lighthouses in the country. Visitors can enjoy a panoramic view in the watchroom gallery after climbing the 199 tower steps. MAC sponsors year round tours including Trolley Tours and Historic District Walking Tours.

Cape May was named one of five National Landmark Cities in the country in 1976. To this day, it is the only city designated this way in the United States. The primary purpose of this designation is to ensure the architectural preservation of these Victorian-era buildings.

The gorgeous beach at Cape May is a delight for beachgoers, surfers, swimmers, and sunbathers. The Travel Channel recognizes it as one of America's top ten beaches. In 2008, the New Jersey Marine Sciences Consortium ranked the Cape May beach fifth in New Jersey. Warm autumn days give visitors an extended taste of summer in Cape May.

Turn the pages and enjoy the excitement of this visual tour of Cape May through the four seasons. Tranquil azure waters of the bay, white crescent waves in the ocean, sandy beaches, historic Victorian architecture, Bed and Breakfasts, and popular restaurants await you.

Tourists gather to visit the shops at Washington Street Mall. Many find Cape May a delight to visit any time of year; autumn brings bright sunshine and comfortable temperatures.

Cape May is fun to explore on foot or by bicycle. A multitude of bicycles and surreys await tourists eager to enjoy the balmy weather and take in the sights around town, with a surrey providing added comfort for these visitors — including a safe storage rack to accommodate their beloved dog.

This miniature golf place on Beach Avenue is just one of the many activities providing tourists and residents hours of fun in the sun.

The sign says it best: the "Best Sandwiches in Town" can be found at the Union Park Restaurant, located at 727 Beach Avenue.

Artists sell original artwork at the beach in front of Surfside Delites and the Arcade, along Beach Avenue. Notice the bicycles lining the road to the beach — that's not an uncommon site.

These homes on Gurney Street were all built alike. Subtle differences of porch details, exterior window treatments, and color produce individuality.

Ornate woodwork decorates a second floor porch while ornate roof decorations adorn all the homes on Gurney.

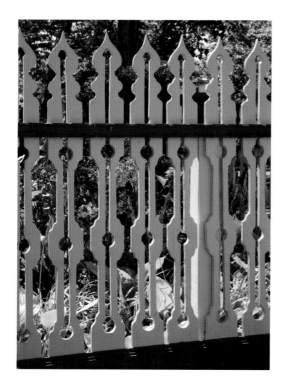

An ornate wooden fencing embellishes a Victorian inspired garden lush with autumn foliage.

11

A crisp, blue sky frames ornate "gingerbread" details of dormer windows and brick chimneys on this Victorian inspired home.

Festive flags beckon visitors to a treasure trove of specialty shops at the Washington Street Mall, including American West and The Toy Shop of Cape May.

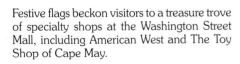

A bicycle decorates this front entry in a festive and unique way while a decorative and functional weathervane adorns a shingled roof.

At 157 feet, the Cape May Lighthouse is a splendid visitor attraction at any time of year. It's located in the Cape May Point State Park.

Tall grasses lead to white sandy beaches and refreshing saltwater seas.

Tranquil blue water forms an inlet surrounded by early autumn landscapes of multihued greens and late blooming flowers.

The tranquil harbor is filled with waiting fishing boats.

Looking over the harbor towards the United States Coast Guard Training Center, Cape May. The Coast Guard has made its home in Cape May for over fifty years.

Pleasure boats docked at the harbor in Cape May.

Gingerbread decorations embellish the porch of this finely appointed Victorian home.

Boldly painted red and green, details pop in crisp white. Many Victorian details decorate this home from the wrought iron cresting on the roof, to the intricate balconies, assorted window shapes, and fancy brackets.

Rich turquoise "pops" on this façade including a fanciful turret with a decorative weathervane.

Arched windows have matching round-headed shutters at the top and are framed by "S" scroll brackets with bold painted edges. This view shows ornate brick chimneys with a fanciful cupola behind.

An array of autumn decorations adorn the front entry of this house including boldly colored chrysanthemums, corn stalks, straw bales, and multi-hued gourds.

Bright turquoise accents embellish this ornate porch. A whimsical Bed and Breakfast sign of brass are miniature sculptures of a bed, coffee cup, and food accoutrements.

This house abounds with sawn-wood ornaments commonly called gingerbread. The handsome balcony is prominent with fanciful balusters. Majestic cresting frames the rooftop and multi-colored shingles decorate the roof with a flower motif.

This grand home at 25 Jackson Street is covered in gingerbread. Autumn flowers of orange, gold, and burgundy fill numerous flower boxes across the porch and balcony. It's now The Virginia Hotel. An intricate balustrade enhances the romantic beauty of the porch.

The Marquis de Lafayette Hotel is conveniently located across the street from the beach.

Many high rise hotels, like the Marquis de Lafayette shown here, provide comfortable vacation getaways along the beach in Cape May.

Skies of deep azure with cottony white clouds frame this majestic seaside resort. A multitude of stairs creates a strong visual impact.

A flock of seagulls fly parallel to the beach on a warm September afternoon.

Warm sunshine and fresh ocean breezes caress the Cape May beaches filled with tourists as they enjoy a taste of summer.

An inviting boardwalk leads to the Cape May-Lewes Ferry visitor center. Here, visitors can lounge and watch the ferry and pleasure craft.

Inset:
The Cape May-Lewes Ferry Terminal entrance welcomes visitors.

Inside the visitors center at Cape May-Lewes Ferry Terminal are many amenities, including an arcade, restaurants, an observation deck, and a gift shop.

The Twin Capes Ferry is receiving cars, recreational vehicles, trucks, and walk-on passengers for the cruise to Lewes, Delaware, the Tanger Outlets, and the Park and Ride Lot where passengers can connect with the Dart Bus System to go to Rehoboth Beach or Ocean City, Maryland.

Entrance to the NAS Wildwood Aviation Museum, 500 Forrestal Road, Cape May Airport.

An exterior view of the Vietnam Veteran Museum on Forrestal Road.

A Coast Guard helicopter and an Apache helicopter on display in the Aviation Museum — they're just some of the many aircraft the museum features.

The Old Grange Building is the only original building at the Historic Cold Spring Village Living History Museum. All of the other buildings were relocated and refurbished to this site.

Historic stocks are on display at Cold Spring Village Living History Museum.

Distinctive historical United States flags decorate the fist floor of the Visitors Center at Historic Cold Spring Village, located at 720 Route 9 South, Cape May.

Visitors can view a historic school at the village as they stroll shaded lanes and step back in time to an Early American South Jersey rural farm community.

Opposite:
The Cold Spring Country Store invites visitors to relax in a rocking chair on the porch after shopping. The Cold Spring Country Store is chock full of gift items including hand-made pottery, corn whisk brooms, knitted and felted handbags, knitted mittens, and natural jams and jellies.

Sheep enjoy their afternoon meal on the 22-acre Early American Open-Air Living History Museum at the Cold Spring Village.

A wagon is stored in the historic barn and is used for weekday wagon rides (weather-permitting).

This beautiful vista includes a water well, wagon, and one of twenty-six historic buildings at the museum.

A historic bell is prominently displayed at the entrance of the Washington Street Mall.

The vintage clock at Cape May Commons.

The surf shop welcomes visitor

The prominent 5 & 10 marquis.

The Salt Water Taffy store has sweets for everyone.

The Jackson Mountain Café at the Commons at Cape May.

Restaurants and stores line the Commons at Cape May.

The Ugly Mug Restaurant has great crab cakes.

A beautiful day at the beach.

Rinsing sandy feet is easy at the beach.

Fun in the sand.

Hot sun, cool water, and wet sand equal summer fun for kids of all ages.

Sunbathers bask in the hot summer breeze.

Catching a wave.

Summer
beaches
welcome July
beachgoers.

Life Guard Rescue Boat.

The Emlen Physick Estate

The Emlen Physick Estate, built in 1879, is one of the finest examples of Victorian "Stick Style" architecture in America. It serves as the only museum of Victorian Living in Cape May, New Jersey. Visitors enjoy tours throughout the year at 1048 Washington Street.

Behind the carriage house at the Emlen Physick Estate, guests can dine in the quaint café with outdoor seating available during the spring, summer, and autumn.

Decorative paint and fine wood details adorn this estate.

Beautiful roses bursting with color and fragrance adorn the estate.

This view of the Museum shows four ornate brick chimneys, gables, and decorative roof brackets.

 44

The four-acre estate has grandly kept grounds inviting visitors all year long.

During the Victorian Festival in September, visitors can
see glass blowing demonstrations at the museum.

Clear autumn skies create a majestic backdrop for the only
museum of Victorian Living in Cape May, New Jersey.

Mature trees and shrubs adorn the extensive estate and clear blue
skies compliment the beauty of the rear view of the museum.

The Southern Mansion

The Southern Mansion, 720 Washington Street, is a luxurious Bed and Breakfast with two acres of gardens. Daily tours are available.

Decorative Victorian details are everywhere in Cape May, including this sign for the Southern Mansion.

Long shadows and bright green grounds welcome
visitors to the gardens at the Southern Mansion.

Arched windows adorn the cupola atop the Southern Mansion with ornately decorated brackets, a multiple color scheme, and a shiny golden finial.

Bright violet flowers still bloom in autumn at the Southern Mansion.

Evergreen wreaths with twinkling lights and bright red bows decorate the street lamps.

Opposite:
The gazebo down town is festively decorated for the winter holidays.

At night the holiday lights shine brilliantly on the gazebo.

A multitude of holiday decorations adorn this lovely Victorian home.

Winter skies frame intricate gingerbread on this delightful home.

Opposite:
This porch is dressed for the holidays with life size carolers and a Christmas tree.

Cape May streets are covered in holiday lights for a festive winter retreat.

Bright white lights frame decorative arches, balconies, and fencing along these homes.

Opposite:
Delightful blue lights outline an ornamental bicycle in front of this quaint home.

This pale turquoise and lavender home is dressed for the holidays with evergreen decorations, lights, and burgundy velvet bows.

Fine Victorian details are on display at this home with a fancy turret, gables, balcony, and decorated porch.

A pink and red color scheme makes a perfect holiday backdrop for festive winter decorations.

Fancy wood gingerbread is abound with Christmas decorations including snow people, a Victorian Santa Claus, lights, garland, and bows.

Countless lights illuminate this wonderful home for the holidays.

Winter nights are filled with lavish holiday lights up and down the streets of Cape May.

Ebony shutters contrast greatly with the pure white background of this pristine home. Finely detailed gingerbread enhances the festive holiday decorations in bright red and green.

Beautiful holiday decorations in rich burgundy, pink, and mauve form a lovely frame for Santa dressed in bright red velvet and white faux fur.

A fully decorated Christmas tree complete with fancy wrapped gifts decorates this lovely front porch.

These homes abound with sparkling holiday lights making a trip to Cape May a festive winter experience.

Evergreen garland with bright red bows decorates this Victorian home in soft blue with white trim and black shutters.

Glistening holiday lights fill the air with joy and wonder.

This gable is decorated with intricate gingerbread and numerous roof brackets.

Swags of garland covered in white lights drape the entrance of this home.

Holiday lights frame a decorative arch leading the *eye* inside this beautifully decorated home.

This detail shows beautiful gingerbread designs on a front porch with a gorgeous holiday wreath with red poinsettias.

Romantically lit tables await diners in this winter wonderland scene at the Lobster House on Schellengers Lane, complete with a glistening Christmas tree, presents, garlands, ribbons, and bows.

Sparkling holiday lights decorate the quaint firehouse.

The Emlen Physick Estate
at Christmastime

The porch welcomes visitors with wooden benches and holiday wreaths.

Holiday lights and fresh pine wreaths decorate the Emlen Physick Estate for the holidays.

An intricate wrought iron bench takes center stage in the entrance area of the Museum.

The masterful fireplace in the formal parlor completes
the grandeur of this room. Decorated with evergreen
garland, ribbon, and greeting cards, the room is ready
to welcome holiday guests.

Vintage canned foods, kitchen gadgets, bottles, and glassware are on display in the main kitchen of the museum.

This Christmas tree is decorated in true Victorian fashion. It is covered in handmade ornaments of paper, home baked cookies, and imported glass ornaments from Germany. Woolworth's began importing these decorations in the 1880s.

Vintage culinary utensils and cookbook are on display atop an antique cabinet.

Winter is a lovely time to visit the Museum. Clear blue
skies and lush evergreens welcome visitors.

Opposite:
Sparkling holiday lights decorate the Museum.

Visitors enjoy this wonderful train display at the carriage house at the Museum.

Festive white lights brightly illuminate the front porch of the Museum.

Holiday lights decorate the Museum and grounds with festive colors for the winter season.

ABOUT THE AUTHORS

Founder, partner and head photographer of JDN Photography Inc., Jack Neith has been photographing for major publications for twenty-five years. His work can be found on covers, in annual reports, and in manufacturers' product brochures and advertisements both nationally and internationally. He is recognized as one of the elite photographers in the United States today.

In 1981, JDN Photography Inc. was established as a commercial photography firm specializing in architectural and interior photography. Located thirty minutes outside of Philadelphia, in Shamong, New Jersey, the company has become recognized for its mastery of balancing light sources. Jack's philosophy is to bring out the ambiance of every room without over lighting it. The end result is a picture that looks like the room as you see it — not a photo with false shadows or reflections. Jack recognizes the challenge different color light sources bring, but with his keen creative eye and technical knowledge he always achieves the results he is looking for.

Jack's inventory of equipment is extensive and includes everything he needs to produce extraordinary photographs using both film and high-resolution digital images. His digital capabilities are state-of-the-art and are kept up-to-date with industry advancements. JDN has won many awards for photo content and imagery.

✶✶✶✶✶✶

Oleta Neith is a writer specializing in books about design. She has decades of experience as a photo stylist for architectural interior photography as well as product photography. Other Schiffer books written by Oleta include *Power Rooms* and *Great Kitchens*.